Food

BANANAS

Louise Spilsbury

Heinemann Library
Chicago, Illinois

© 2002 Heinemann Library
a division of Reed Elsevier Inc.
Chicago, Illinois

Customer Service 888-454-2279

Visit our website at www.heinemannlibrary.com

Designed by Celia Floyd
Illustrated by Alan Fraser and Jeff Edwards
Originated by Ambassador Litho
Printed in Hong Kong/China by South China Printing Co.

06 05 04 03
10 9 8 7 6 5 4 3 2 1
Library of Congress Cataloging-in-Publication Data
Spilsbury, Louise.
   Bananas / Louise Spilsbury.
      v. cm. -- (Food)
Includes index.
Contents: What are bananas? -- Kinds of bananas -- In the past -- Around the world -- Banana plants -- Growing bananas -- Picking and washing -- Sorting and packing -- Bananas to us -- Eating bananas -- Good for you -- Healthy eating -- Banana milkshake recipe.
   ISBN 1-58810-615-2 (HC), 1-4034-4046-8 (Pbk.)
   1. Cookery (Bananas)--Juvenile literature. 2. Bananas--Juvenile literature. [1. Bananas.] I. Title. II. Series.
   TX813.B3 S65 2002
   641.6'4772--dc21
                                    2002000471

Acknowledgments
The author and publishers are grateful to the following for permission to reproduce copyright material: pp. 4, 9, 11, 14, 15, 16, 17, 18, 19, 25 Corbis; pp. 5, 21 Holt Studios International; p. 6 Photodisc; p. 7 Visuals Unlimited/Jack Ballard; p. 8 Oxford Scientific Films/Richard Davies; p. 12 Ardea London/Liz Bomford; p. 13 Ardea London/David Dixon; p. 20 Garden and Wildlife Matters; p. 22 Gareth Boden; pp. 23, 28, 29 (top and bottom) Liz Eddison; p. 24 Stone.

Cover photograph: Gareth Boden.

Some words are shown in bold, **like this.** You can find out what they mean by looking in the glossary.

Contents

What Are Bananas?

Bananas are a kind of **fruit** that we can eat. A fruit is a part of a plant. Bananas are one of the most popular fruits in the world.

Bananas do not grow on trees. They grow on banana plants. Farmers grow lots of banana plants together on **plantations** like this one.

Kinds of Bananas

There are hundreds of different kinds of bananas in the world. The kind we usually see at the grocery store is the common yellow banana.

Other kinds of bananas look and taste different. They may be different colors, shapes, and sizes. Some bananas are cooked before eating.

In the Past

The first banana plants grew in Malaysia more than 4,000 years ago. Many different kinds of bananas still grow in Malaysia today.

Lots of the bananas we eat today come from islands in the Caribbean Sea. Spanish **explorers** first grew banana plants there 500 years ago.

Around the World

Bananas grow in **tropical** countries where it is sunny and it rains a lot. This map of the world shows you where most banana plants grow.

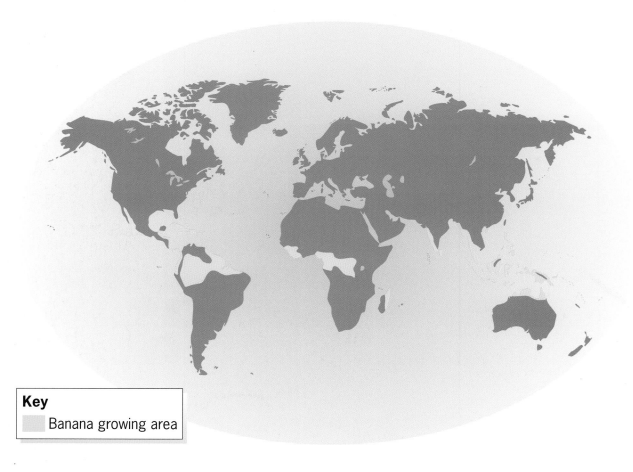

Key
Banana growing area

Some people use the leaves of the banana plant, as well as eating the **fruit.** In China, people use the leaves to make mats, to cover roofs, and to wrap food.

Banana Plants

Banana plants grow from an underground **stem.** Long leaves grow up from the stem. The bases of the leaves grow so tightly together that they look like a **tree trunk.**

leaves

base of the leaves

Bananas grow from a huge **stalk** of flowers. This comes from the middle of the plant. Farmers call bananas "fingers." They call the bunches "hands."

flower

finger

hand

Growing Bananas

In some places, workers put big plastic bags over the tiny bananas. This keeps birds and **insects** from eating them.

Some people feed their banana plants with **fertilizers** to help them grow well. People also use sprays to keep the plants from getting **diseases.**

Picking and Washing

Bananas take about three months to grow. Workers pick them before they are **ripe,** when they are still green. They cut the whole **stalk** off the plant.

Then workers cut the green bananas into bunches. They wash the bananas in huge tubs of cold water. This cleans any dirt off the **fruit.**

Sorting and Packing

Workers check the bananas and throw away any bad ones. They put a sticker on each banana to tell **consumers** where they come from.

Workers pack the bananas into boxes.
These boxes keep the bananas from
being **damaged** while they travel
from the **plantation** to the stores.

19

Bananas to Us

Some bananas are sold in the country where they grew. Others are **exported** to different countries. They travel on ships in containers that are like giant fridges. This helps keep them fresh.

Before bananas arrive at the store, they go to a ripening center. This has warm rooms that make the bananas **ripe.** Bananas turn yellow when ripe.

Eating Bananas

Most people eat bananas **raw.** You just take off the **peel** and eat the **fruit** inside. Some people like to put sliced bananas on their cereal.

Bananas also taste good made into muffins, cakes, breads, or yogurt. Some people also eat banana **products** such as banana chips or **dried** bananas.

Good for You

Bananas are good for you. They contain **vitamins.** Vitamins help your body to grow and protect you from **disease.**

Bananas contain **carbohydrates** too. Carbohydrates help to fill you up and give you lots of **energy.** Runners often eat bananas to keep them going during a long race.

Healthy Eating

The food guide **pyramid** shows how much of each different kind of food you should eat every day.

All of the food groups are important, but your body needs more of some foods than others.

You should eat more of the foods at the bottom and the middle of the pyramid. You should eat less of the foods at the top.

Bananas are in the **fruit** group. Your body needs two servings of foods in the fruit group each day.

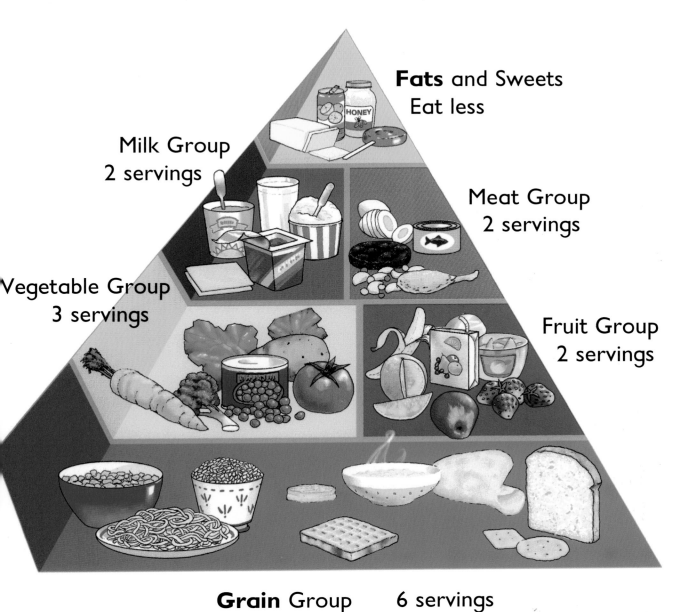

Fats and Sweets
Eat less

Milk Group
2 servings

Meat Group
2 servings

Vegetable Group
3 servings

Fruit Group
2 servings

Grain Group   6 servings

Based on the Food Guide Pyramid for Young Children, U.S. Department of
Agriculture, Center for Nutrition Policy and Promotion, March 1999.

27

Banana Milkshake Recipe

1. Take the banana out of its **peel** and put it into a blender.

2. Add the milk, vanilla ice cream, and lemon juice.

You will need:
- 1 banana
- 1 cup (225 ml) milk
- 3 scoops of vanilla ice cream
- 1 teaspoon (5 ml) lemon juice

Ask an adult to help you!

3. Put the lid onto the blender and ask an adult to turn it on for one minute.

4. Pour the milkshake into glasses and enjoy!

Glossary

carbohydrate   part of food that the body uses to get energy

consumer   person who buys things that he or she needs or wants, like food

damage   to cause harm to something

disease   sickness that can harm plants or animals

dried   having had all the water removed before packing

energy   to be able and strong enough to do things

explorer   person who travels to an unknown land to find out more about it

export   to send something to another country to be sold

fat   part of some foods that the body uses to get energy and to keep warm

fertilizer   spray or powder that helps plants grow bigger and produce more fruit

fruit   part of a plant that grows around the seeds

grain   seed of a cereal plant

insect   tiny creature with six legs

peel   thin outer layer of a fruit

30

plantation   place where lots of banana plants grow together

product   something that is made to be sold

pyramid   shape with a flat bottom and three sides with edges that come to a point

raw   not cooked

ripe   completely grown and ready to eat

stalk   part of a plant from which flowers grow

stem   part of plant that holds leaves and flowers up above the ground

tree trunk   large woody stem of a tree

tropical   lying near the Equator. Tropical areas are usually hot and humid.

vitamin   something that the body needs to grow and stay healthy

More Books to Read

Fox, Mary Virginia. *Costa Rica*. Chicago: Heinemann Library, 2001.

Royston, Angela. *Eat Well*. Chicago: Heinemann Library, 1999.

Royston, Angela. *Flowers, Fruits and Seeds*. Chicago: Heinemann Library, 1999.

Index